Feng Shui

the way to anyone's heart is through the stomach

in the kitchen

THE INFLUENCE OF CHI

The atmosphere in the kitchen during food preparation is important. Ideally, food should be prepared in a light, harmonious atmosphere. Each cooking process changes the chi, the life energy of a nutrient. That is why the energy centre of a house or apartment is the kitchen or, in former times, the hearth. The quality and oscillations of the food being prepared in this area should build up the members of the family, guaranteeing them optimum health and life force. Of all the equipment and areas in the kitchen, the location of the cooker is the most important.

COOKER AGAINST THE WALL

In intimate situations, we love a protected place, ideally somewhere where our back is protected. Cooking can be compared with one of these situations. After all, the idea is that the cook, from his or her position of strength, produces an agreeable meal that gives us lots of energy, and so the best position for the cooker is one that gives you a vantage point of your kitchen.

The best way of achieving this ideal is by investing in an island. Not only does this give you the best view over the kitchen, but it also promotes your wellbeing and enables you to communicate with family and friends while cooking.

100 PERCENT CHI - MOOD IS THE KEY

High-quality food that is full of energy is much more than the sum of its ingredients. The nutrients in the food change during the cooking process, and while they are changing they absorb the vibrations emitting from a happy and contented cook just as much as those from an unquiet atmosphere. So you should never have your back to the door while you are cooking, as you are then unable to see who is approaching you. It helps if you hang a mirror or reflective metal surface behind the cooker, as this will give you a clear view of who is in the kitchen. It also "opens up" the wall optically, and this gives a pleasing impression of depth. Another advantage: the mirror "doubles" the food, and so it increases the potential chi, which, in the world of feng shui, is especially beneficial to fortune and finance.

If the mirror solution is not feasible in your kitchen, then hang some wind chimes near the kitchen door. This will make you feel safe, since you will then always be able to hear if someone is entering the kitchen behind you.

POWER FOR THE KITCHEN

The ideal kitchen is light, bright, and cheerfully decorated. The best wall colours are gently toned whites, yellows, and earth tones. As fresh air is also an important source of good chi, the kitchen should be aired regularly. Overall, it should radiate an animating, spring-like liveliness. Fresh pot plants are good, as is a bowl of fruit, brimming with market-fresh delicacies. Watch how you stand in front of the cooker. The area before your head must be clear. Cumbersome extractor hoods are like the proverbial wooden plank or brick wall. The best extractors are those that are small, with rounded corners.

Ceiling beams have a similar effect. In order to keep oppressive influences away from the cooker and dining table, any beams should be painted in light colours or – ideally – integrated in the ceiling. The least that can be done is to drape a cloth beneath them to dissolve any negative influences.

The best ideas are
and help to keep energy flowing freely
always the simplest

CUTTING CORNERS

When eating, avoid the corners of your table, since sharp corners on your furniture can cause restlessness or quarrels. The furniture in sitting areas, or areas that you frequently pass through or spend time in, should be gently rounded to solve this problem. In accordance with the controlling cycle of the Five Elements, the sink, washing machine, refrigerator, and dishwasher (governed by water) should never be placed next to the cooker (governed by fire). This water-fire conflict can be solved with "wood". Ideally, plan a small cupboard as a divider between the "fighters", fire and water, or else symbolize the distinction by hanging a wooden spoon on the wall between two conflicting machines.

THE OPTIMUM EATING PLACE

Energy-laden food is best eaten in a light, comfortable atmosphere, and so it is essential that the dining corner or room be as harmonious in every respect as possible. The ideal table shape is round, but oval, square, rectangular, and octangular are also favourable. Three cornered tables, irregular surfaces, and tables with angled corners are considered "quarrelsome". A tablecloth will help to soften the corners, and a vase of fresh flowers, or a circular ornament in the middle of the table will help to "smooth things over". Friendly pictures and light colours add to the beauty of the room. Banish any unloved antiques, uncomfortable chairs, loud radios and TVs, irritating objects, and other stress factors from the dining room. The gap in an extending table will also upset the atmosphere, and so should be "bridged" with a cloth, a suitably shaped dish, or even a vase.

VEGETABLES: A DIFFERENT CUT

How you cut fruit, vegetables, and other foods affects both the energy content and the character of the food. Try it and see: cut carrots, leeks, or celery in two different ways, one half as you would normally, and the other in diagonals, dice, or strips. Each different shape has a living tension inside it – from the front and from behind, or the Yin and the Yang. If you cut vegetables at sharp right angles, they lose this tension and

contain less chi. And you will notice that in the flavour.

A Clean Cut

Looking after your "tools" properly is as important as cleanliness and order. The smooth cut of a sharp knife energizes the food with clarity and precision. Loving preparation by hand gives the food favourable chi vibrations – different from those achieved with kitchen machines, whose high-speed perfection always lacks that "certain something".

Your Attitude is Extremely Important

Your own personal attitude is the most important thing in everything you do. A meal that has been prepared with love and devotion is infinitely more digestible than one that may be technically perfect, but which has been prepared under stress and with resentment. So go with the flow, and choose the form of preparation that suits the available time. That way, your meals will always have twice the chi.

The five-

a dynamic cycle

element model

LET THE ENERGY FLOW INTO YOU

Just as a feng shui master will bring the objects around you into the most harmonious chi flow, you can use the five-element kitchen to benefit your body and your soul.

Chinese dietetics, one aspect of Traditional Chinese Medicine (TCM), deals primarily with the existing energy in the food and the ability of the human organism to utilize this energy. Life means energy, and living processes always represent dynamic ratios of balance. In a high-energy diet, calories, protein, fat, carbohydrates, vitamins, and trace elements are of secondary importance. The effects of a dish on the person are the primary consideration. The thermionics – the amount of Yin/cold and Yang/heat that the nutrients create in the body – are particularly important to create the right energy for your body. If the body's energy is right, then your diet is balanced. Each element (corresponding to an organ) must receive the right amount of energy.

Each food harmonizes with a particular element. Depending on the flavour, it provides energy for a particular element, and depending on the thermionics, it cools or warms the element and the appropriate organ. If the five elements in your diet are balanced, each element will receive sufficient energy.

However, if an element is deficient, this can be put right by altering your choice of food to include more (or less) heating or warming nutrients. The element with the deficiency needs a warming food, such as vinegar, leeks, grilled meat, nuts, chicken, or raspberries. An element with excess or blocked energy needs refreshment or cooling, for example by eating more lettuce, apples, wheat, dairy products, long-grain rice, or plaice.

The more "flames" are burning in the kitchen, the greater the amount of energy that is transferred to the food you are preparing. The more energy your body has, the more efficiently you will be able to perform your daily duties and increase your wellbeing. The greater your wellbeing, the more nourishing your food will be, and the more easily your energy becomes balanced.

CLASSIFICATION

The elements wood, fire, earth, metal, and water are the building stones of everything. The following table shows that each element possesses different features. Each element equates to a pair of organs, one hollow organ and one that is used for storage, and their functions; each also relates to one sensory organ, one state of emotion, one body tissue, one season, one colour, one virtue, and one odour.

THE MAIN CLASSIFICATIONS OF THE FIVE ELEMENTS

	WOOD	FIRE	EARTH	METAL	WATER
Organ	liver/gall bladder	heart/small intestine	spleen-pancreas/ stomach	lung/large intestine	kidney/ bladder
Flavour	sour	bitter	sweet	spicy	salty
Sensory organ ("opener")	eye	tongue	mouth	nose	ear
Season	spring	summer	harvest, late summer	fall	winter
Climate	wind	heat	humidity	dryness	cold
Emotion	anger	pleasure	worry	sadness	fear
Tissue	muscles	blood vessels	tissue	skin	bones
Colour	blue-green	red	yellow	white/light grey	blue/black
Smell	rancid	burnt	aromatic	fishy	rotting
Direction	east	south	middle	west	north
Virtue	goodness	morality	trust	honesty	wisdom
Expression of feeling	screaming	laughing	singing	crying	sighing

Between the

tank up on new energy for increased wellbeing

elements

AN ELEMENT FOR EACH ORGAN

Every organ in your body corresponds to a flavour. Foods with this type of flavour also feed the organ, the corresponding tissue, the appropriate sense, and an emotion. "Wine makes merry" – the liver, which is associated with wood, relaxes; anger and tension dissolve, and the dynamic force of spring develops to give you activity and fun. An old German proverb tells us that "what's bitter in the mouth is good for the heart". In five-element eating, bitter foods support the cardio-circulatory system. These foods give your fire element a balanced chi flow, and at the same time harmonize the associated areas. Naturally sweet foods support your earth element. The more natural sweetness there is in your diet, such as from carrots, pasta, and potatoes, the more power you will feel and the more you will be able to dispense with sugary foods. Spicy foods feed your metal element. Their influence is beneficial to the chi flow through your body and soul. Finally, the "salt of life" is associated with the water element. The Chinese believe that the

kidneys (the organs of the water element) store the chi force for your entire life, and they should therefore be well looked after.

THE FEEDING CYCLE

The elements are all linked together in a dynamic cycle, and within it each element has its own fixed place and role. Moving in a clockwise direction, each element "feeds" the next one:

Through its flavour, every nutrient can be allocated to an element. And each element that you add to your food supports your energy on every level. Furthermore, each

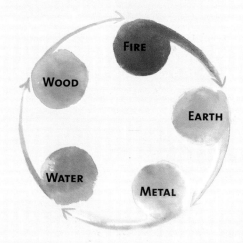

element controls the next-but-one element in a clockwise cycle.

COOKING ACCORDING TO THE CYCLE

You will receive energy-rich food by providing every element with its corresponding nutrient, and its specific flavour, when you cook. In the five-element cycle, you add the individual ingredients to your dish successively. With each circulation you increase the overall chi in your meal. The recipes in this book all follow this cycle, so it is important that you keep to the sequence of ingredients. If your body has a deficiency, surplus, or blockage of energy in a particular area, you can balance it out again by eating the appropriate foods.

An organ that has an energy deficiency (= yin state) needs warming foods of the corresponding element (yang-based food). An organ that has a blockage or surplus of energy (= yang state) will be harmonized by cooling foods of the corresponding element (yin-based food). The individual recipes give their yin and yang structure.

YIN OR YANG IN BALANCE

To determine whether your food is giving you enough energy, ask yourself three simple questions after every meal. Your (honest!) answers will indicate whether your overall energy is balanced.

1. Do I really feel full of energy and satisfied?
2. Do I feel a pleasant warmth in my whole body?
3. Am I sufficiently full and unlikely to be thinking of food for the next 3–4 hours?

If you answer no to any of these questions, you can give your body more physical and mental energy with your food.

To make it easier for you to cook in a cycle, the ingredients are all listed by element. These are the abbreviations used in the recipes:

* (Wd) Wood
* (F) Fire
* (E) Earth
* (M) Metal
* (W) Water

Power

increased harmony, enjoyment, and wellbeing

week

IMPROVE YOUR BALANCE
WEEK BY WEEK

You can do something good for each one of your elements (ie organs) on every day of the week. The kidneys are associated with the water element, and the liver with the wood element. Because of the special roles these two organs play in metabolizing your food, they deserve extra care, so once every element has been served they are given an extra day as a bonus.

For ease of use, the chapters in this book are divided into the five elements. This means that you can select dishes to suit the season, for example, by choosing the wood element in spring, the fire element in summer, the earth element in the humid late summer, the metal element in the autumn, and the water element in winter. Any organ that is particularly stressed can be given new chi. If, for example, you are having problems with your liver and gall bladder, choose recipes from the "wood" chapter. If you want to liven up your heart and circulation, the recipes in the "fire" chapter are ideal. Anyone who is seeking harmony, relaxation, and the chance to catch their breath, should turn to the "wood" chapter. If you are worried, you will find some helpful recipes in the "metal" chapter.

Compile your high-energy menu by eating a combination of elements; for example, choose a "fire" starter and main course, and a "wood" dessert.

It's a good idea to begin the day with a "pick-me-up" from the wood element for breakfast. Satisfy your mid-morning appetite with a "fiery" snack. Strengthen yourself at midday with an "earth" meal. In the afternoon, eat a little something from the "metal" section, and later a warming, energy-laden evening meal from the "water" chapter.

Once you have experienced how full of energy you can feel by trying a few of the recipes in this book, you are sure to think of lots of other ways of enjoying this sensible way of increasing your wellbeing. Your favourite recipes will be even tastier. RECOMMENDATION: Use organic produce wherever possible. If you wish to avoid genetically modified (GM) foods, read any labels with care and select certified organic produce, as this is not produced from GM ingredients.

Week Plan

Monday

* Toasted Oat Muesli * Sweet-boiled Water with cardamom seeds
* Buckwheat with Sage * Sweet-boiled Water
* Brussels Sprouts with Crushed Nutmeg * 1 glass of Bordeaux (Graves)

Tuesday

* Millet Salad with Asparagus and Capers * Sweet-boiled Water with aniseed
* Linguine with Vegetable Strips * Sweet-boiled Water
* Lamb's Lettuce with Avocado and Mango * 1 glass of dry Rheingauer Auslese

Wednesday

* Miso Soup with Horseradish and Coriander * Sweet-boiled Water with star anise
* Spicy Chicken Kebabs * Sweet-boiled Water
* Celeriac strips on Turnips * 1 glass of Sake

Thursday

* Chickpea Purée with Sesame on toasted white bread * Sweet-boiled Water with soy sauce * Lentil Soup with Rosemary * Sweet-boiled Water with fruit vinegar
* Catfish in Root Vegetable Stock * 1 glass of Manzanilla sherry

Friday

* Miso Soup with Parsley * Sweet-boiled Water with fruit vinegar
* Dandelion Salad with Grapefruit * Sweet-boiled Water * Duck Livers on Redcurrants * 1 glass of white wine (white Burgundy, dry Spätlese)

Saturday

* Terrine of Smoked Trout with bread * Sweet-boiled Water with sea vegetables
* Fennel Purée with Eggplant Chips * Sweet-boiled Water
* Skin-fried Perch * 1 glass of white wine (Burgundy 1er cru)

Sunday

* Hazelnut and Parsley Pâté on bread * Sweet-boiled Water
* Green Spelt Grain Risotto with Rocket * 1 glass of white wine
* Chard Vegetables * 1 glass of white wine

Cucumber

delicious as a starter

Salad with

or side dish

Coriander

Serves 2: • sea salt • 2 cucumbers • 2 tbsp white wine vinegar • pinch of ground paprika • pinch of cane sugar • 1 carrot • 1 tbsp olive oil • pinch of curry powder • 10 coriander seeds • 1 garlic clove

Measure 2 teaspoons of sea salt (W) into a bowl. Peel the cucumber (Wd) and slice thinly, then cut into strips. Combine well and leave to stand for 10 minutes. Squeeze out, and pour away the liquid. Add the vinegar (Wd), ground paprika (F), and cane sugar (E). Wash the carrot (E), peel, and grate thinly onto the cucumber. Add the olive oil (E), curry powder (M), and coriander seeds (M). Peel the garlic (M), chop finely, and add to the rest of the ingredients. Combine well and season with a little salt (W).

power YIN-PROMOTING

Dandelion Salad

removes blockages and refreshes

with Grapefruit

Serves 2: • 500 g (1 lb 2 oz) dandelion leaves • 8 cherry tomatoes • 2 tbsp wine vinegar • 1 grapefruit

• 2 tbsp wheat flakes • 2 soft-boiled egg yolks • 2 tbsp cream • 2 tbsp olive oil • 1 tsp mustard

• 1 tbsp water • salt

Wash the dandelion (Wd) and chop. Wash the cherry tomatoes (Wd), halve, and remove the core

and seeds. Combine both with the vinegar (Wd). Peel the grapefruit (Wd), removing the white pith

as well. Cut out the fruit segments and add to the salad. Toast the wheat flakes (F). Stir into the

salad with the egg yolks (E), cream (E), olive oil (E), mustard (M), water (W), and a pinch of salt (W).

YIN-PROMOTING

Tomatoes with

relaxes the liver when stressed

Apple Stuffing

Serves 2: • 4 tomatoes • ¹/₂ apple (Cox's or similar) • 2 tbsp balsamic vinegar • 4 tsp olive paste • pinch

of ground paprika • 4 tsp breadcrumbs • 1 tsp butter • pepper • sea salt • lemon juice

Wash the tomatoes (Wd) and cut off the tops. Scoop out the seeds, reserving the juice. Chop the

flesh and spoon into the tomatoes. Peel the apples (Wd), chop, and add to the chopped tomatoes

with the vinegar. Preheat the oven to 150 °C (300 °F). Place 1 tsp olive paste (F), paprika (F), and 1 tsp

breadcrumbs (E) into each tomato. Place the tomatoes in a dish with a little butter (E), sprinkle

with some pepper (M) and salt (W). Drizzle over the tomato juice (Wd) and lemon juice (Wd). Bake

in the middle of the oven for 15 minutes (F). **YIN-PROMOTING**

Steamed Chard

refreshes an over-stressed liver

Trim and wash the chard (Wd), then cut into strips and place in a saucepan with the wine. Season with paprika (F). Wash and peel the carrot (E), and grate finely over the chard. Wash and dry the orange, then grate the rind with a zester and add to the vegetables. Trim and wash the spring onions (M), slice diagonally, and also add to the vegetables. Squeeze the juice from the orange. Pour the water (W) and the juice (Wd) into the saucepan. Cover with a lid and steam gently over a low heat (F) for 10 minutes. Spoon into a heatproof dish with a slotted spoon, and season with paprika (F). Preheat the oven to 160 °C (325 °F).

Reduce the vegetable cooking liquid to about 6 tablespoons. Pour the cream (E) over the chard, grate over the cheese (E), and sprinkle over the curry powder (M). Pour over the vegetable liquid (W) and lemon juice (Wd), and bake in the middle of the oven (F) until the cheese has melted.

Serves 2:

1 bunch of chard
glass of white wine
pinch of ground paprika
1 carrot
1 unwaxed orange
bunch of spring onions
2 tbsp water
2 tbsp cream
70 g (2¹/₂ oz) Appenzeller cheese
pinch of curry powder
1 tbsp lemon juice

Chard

The acid contained in this vitalizing green vegetable nourishes the liver and the gall bladder. It is refreshing and provides essential juices. Yin-promoting foods that taste sour remove blockages and help us to "digest" anger and irritation.

YIN

PROMOTING

power

Marinated Leeks

goes well with cold roast meats or mild goat's cheese

with Tarragon

Serves 2:

2 leeks
250 ml (10 fl oz) white wine
bunch of tarragon
4 juniper berries
3 tbsp olive oil
pepper
sea salt
3 tbsp vegetable stock
rind of 1 unwaxed lemon
2 pinches ground paprika
pinch of dried sugar cane juice
(from a health-food store)
1 tsp Dijon mustard

Trim the leek (Wd), cut in half if necessary, and wash. Cut each half into three equal-sized pieces, and place upright in a screw-top jar. Cover with white wine (Wd). Wash and shake dry the tarragon (Wd), and chop finely. Add to the leeks, together with the juniper berries (F), 2 tablespoons of oil (E), pepper (M), salt (W), vegetable stock (W), lemon rind (Wd), ground paprika (F), dried sugar cane juice (E), and mustard (M). Place the lid on the jar, tighten, and shake well. Leave the jar at room temperature for a few hours, or place in the refrigerator for 2–3 days. Preheat the oven to 70 °C (160 °F). Place the leeks and the marinade in a saucepan, and simmer gently over a low heat (F) for about 5 minutes. Remove the leeks, and keep warm in the oven. Meanwhile, reduce the cooking liquid by half, sprinkle over the remaining oil (E), then season with pepper (M) and pour over the leeks (W).

power

YANG-PROMOTING

Duck Livers on

provides juice for the liver

Redcurrants

Serves 2:
2 duck livers
200 g (7 oz) redcurrants
1 carrot
1 garlic clove
1/2 tbsp unsalted butter
pepper
1 tsp sesame seeds
1/2 tsp ground paprika
1–2 tbsp cream
pinch of curry powder
sea salt

Wash the livers, and pat dry with paper towels. Preheat the oven to 70 °C/160 °F. Wash the redcurrants (Wd), reserving two whole stalks as garnish, and remove the remaining currants from the stalks. Wash and peel the carrot, and cut into thin strips. Peel the garlic clove and cut in half. Heat a frying pan (F), slowly melt the butter (E), and season with pepper (M). Fry the garlic (M), sesame seeds (W), and the livers (Wd) for 5 minutes on both sides. Place the livers in the oven to keep warm. Add the redcurrants to the sesame seeds (W) in the frying pan, heat briefly, then season with the ground paprika (F). Add the carrot (E). Stir in the cream (E) and simmer gently for 2 minutes. Season with curry powder (M) and salt (W). Divide the sauce between two plates, place the livers on the sauce, and garnish with the reserved redcurrants.

Redcurrants

The berries are full of acid and contain lots of water. They provide lots of liquid for the body, which relieves and relaxes the liver and the gall bladder.

power

Yin

PROMOTING

Green Spelt Grain

lots of energy for the liver

Risotto with Rocket

Serves 2: • 1 carrot • 1 courgette (zucchini) • 200 g (7 oz) unripe spelt grain • pepper • 600 ml (24 fl oz) vegetable stock
• 1 unwaxed lemon • bunch of rocket • ground paprika • 1 tbsp unsalted butter • mustard • salt • balsamic vinegar

Peel the carrot. Cut the carrot and the courgette lengthwise into thin slices, then cut crosswise
into strips. Toast the spelt grain (E). Add the vegetables (E), season with pepper (M), and pour over
the vegetable stock (W). Cut off a piece of the lemon rind (Wd) and add. Cook everything for 25 to
30 minutes. Wash the rocket (F), and shake dry, then chop and add to the pan. Add the ground
paprika (F), butter (E), mustard (M), salt (W), and a little vinegar (Wd), and stir.

power

YANG-PROMOTING

WOOD ELEMENT

Hazelnut and

deliciously creamy sandwich topping

Parsley Pâté

Serves 2: • 100 g (3 ¹/₂ oz) hazelnuts • 100 g (3 ¹/₂ oz) sesame seeds • bunch of flat-leafed
parsley • pinch of ground paprika • 1 tbsp olive oil • pinch of ground cinnamon • sea salt •
lemon juice

Place the hazelnuts (Wd) and the sesame seeds (Wd) in a blender. Wash and shake
dry the parsley (Wd), and remove the leaves from the stalks. Place in the blender with
the ground paprika (F), olive oil (E), ground cinnamon (M), salt (W), and lemon juice
(Wd), and blend until you have a smooth paste.

power

YANG-PROMOTING

Raspberry

light, smooth, and creamy

Crème

Wash and pick over the raspberries (Wd), and, reserving a few for garnish, place them in a saucepan. Ad the red wine (F) and the cocoa powder (F), and heat. Meanwhile, slit open the vanilla pod (E), remove the pulp with a knife, and finely chop the pod. Add to the raspberries with the dried sugar cane juice, and simmer gently over a medium heat for about 20 minutes until reduced by half. Place the gelatine (E) and the peppercorns (M) in a bowl of water to soften. Squeeze out the gelatine, and add to the raspberries with the peppercorns to dissolve. Place the raspberries in a bowl in icy water to cool. Whip the cream (W), and carefully combine with the raspberries. Place the crème in the refrigerator for about 3 hours to chill. Serve in dishes, and garnish with the mint (Wd) and the reserved raspberries.

Serves 2:

500 g (1 lb 2 oz) raspberries
¹/₂ glass of red wine
pinch of cocoa powder
1 vanilla pod
1 tbsp dried sugar cane juice
(from a health-food store)
4 leaves of gelatine
2 peppercorns
300 ml (12 fl oz) whipping cream
mint for garnishing

power
YANG-PROMOTING

Red Camargue Rice
lifts the mood
with Amarone

Place the Camargue rice (F) in a saucepan and dry roast over a medium heat (F) for 10 minutes, stirring continuously. Remove the saucepan from the heat, then pour over the Amarone (F), add the butter (E), and bring to a boil over a low heat. Trim and wash the mushrooms (E), then slice and add to the saucepan. Season with pepper (M) and curry powder (M). Pour over the vegetable stock (W). Cook the risotto for 25 minutes. Season with salt (W) and a few dashes of lemon juice (Wd). Spoon onto plates or into bowls, then garnish with basil leaves and serve.

Serves 2:

200 g (7 oz) red Camargue rice
300 ml (12 fl oz) Amarone wine
1 tbsp unsalted butter
200 g (7 oz) brown mushrooms
pepper
pinch of curry powder
120 ml (5 fl oz) vegetable stock
sea salt
lemon juice
fresh basil

An aromatic drop

Amarone is a very strong, dry red wine from the Veneto region in Italy. It is made from dried grapes and is available from any good wine merchant.

YIN

PROMOTING

Toasted Oat

with pear and raisins for natural sweetness

Muesli

Serves 2: • 100 g (3 $^1/_2$ oz) oats • 1 Williams pear • 2 tsp unsalted butter • 2 tbsp cream • 50 g (1 $^3/_4$ oz) raisins • pinch of ground cinnamon • sea salt • orange juice • pinch of cocoa powder

Dry-fry the oats (F) over a medium heat for about 5 minutes. Peel and chop the pear (E). Add the butter (E), cream (E), pear and raisins (E) to the oats, and stir. Cover with a lid and simmer over a low heat for 7 minutes. Season with ground cinnamon (M), salt (W), a little orange juice (Wd), and cocoa powder (F).

power

YIN-PROMOTING

Rocket Salad with

provides essential juices for the heart

a Cider Dressing

Serves 2: • 1 courgette (zucchini) • 1 carrot • 2 bunches of rocket • 1 onion • 200 ml (7 fl oz) cider • pepper • 2 tbsp vegetable stock • sea salt • 1 tbsp crème fraîche • pinch of ground paprika

Wash and trim the courgette and the carrot, and peel the carrot. Cut both lengthwise into slices, then crosswise into strips. Wash and drain the rocket, then shred. Peel and dice the onion. Bring the cider (Wd) to a boil. Place the rocket (F), sliced vegetables (E), and the onion (M) in the cider, and season with pepper (M). Pour over the stock (W), simmer for 3 minutes, and then season with salt (W). Stir in the crème fraîche, and sprinkle over the ground paprika (F).

power

YIN-PROMOTING

Chicory with
with juices for the heart
Goat's Cheese

Wash and halve the chicory, and remove the core. Bring 500 ml (20 fl oz) water (W) to a boil with the vinegar (Wd), and blanch the chicory (F) for about 3 minutes. Remove the chicory and drain. Place in an ovenproof dish, and sprinkle over the ground paprika (F). Preheat the oven to 150 °C (300 °F).

Spread 1 teaspoon of pesto (F) over each chicory half. Dot with the butter (F), then sprinkle over the breadcrumbs (E) and season with the pepper (M). Peel the shallot (M), slice thinly, and sprinkle over the chicory. Crumble the cheese (W) over the chicory. Cut 2 strips of rind from the lemon (Wd), then cut these into long, thin strips, and sprinkle over the cheese. Grate the cucumber (Wd) into thin slices, and sprinkle over the cheese. Bake in the middle of the oven for about 15 minutes (F).

Serves 2:

- 2 heads of chicory
- 1 tsp white wine vinegar
- pinch of ground paprika
- 4 tsp pesto (ready-made)
- 1 tbsp unsalted butter
- 2 tbsp breadcrumbs
- pepper
- 1 shallot
- 100 g (3 ¹/₂ oz) goat's cheese or Roquefort
- 1 unwaxed lemon
- 1 small cucumber

Chicory

Its bitter flavour and high water content provide plenty of liquid for the fire element – heart and small intestine – as well as removing blockages and increasing wellbeing.

YIN

PROMOTING

Saddle of Lamb
with crispy crackling and tender meat
with Rosemary

Serves 2:
800 g (1 lb 12 oz) saddle of lamb, with fat and on the bone (ask your butcher to remove)
sprig of rosemary
1 tbsp lemon juice
1 carrot
1 garlic clove
1 onion
400 g (³/₄ lb) small potatoes
4 juniper berries
2 cloves
pepper
2 tbsp chopped tomatoes

Score the fatty layer of the meat (F). Preheat the oven to 160 °C/350 °F. Heat a large frying pan over medium heat. Place the meat, fat side down, in the pan, and sprinkle over the rosemary (F). Fry the meat for 12–15 minutes, then turn. Turn off the heat, leaving the pan on the hob for about another 10 minutes. Remove the meat and leave to cool. If you want to eat less fat, remove the skin and the fat, and place in the oven at 160 °C (320 °F), in the frying pan, to render. Then reduce the oven temperature to 70 °C (160 °F).

Meanwhile, pour the lemon juice (Wd) into 1.5 litres (2 pints) of water, and bring to a boil (F). Wash and peel the carrot. Peel the garlic and the onion. Thoroughly wash the potatoes. Add the lamb bone (F), juniper berries (F), carrots (E), potatoes (E), garlic (M), onion (M), and cloves (M) to the water, and cook gently for about 20 minutes, removing any scum with a slotted spoon.

Peel the potatoes and fry in the rendered fat. Remove and place in the oven with the lamb to keep warm. Season the cooking juices with pepper (M), then pour over some stock (W) and bring to a boil. Bind with the tomatoes (Wd). Arrange the meat on plates and serve with the sauce.

power
YANG-PROMOTING

Brussels Sprouts with

with a clever combination of spices

Crushed Nutmeg

Trim, wash, and halve the Brussels sprouts. Crush the nutmeg with a knife.

Heat a pan over a low heat (F). Place the crushed nutmeg (F), then the sprouts (F), and finally the butter (E) in the pan.

Braise the sprouts over a low heat for about 10 minutes, stirring frequently.

Season the sprouts with a pinch each of curry powder (M) and mustard powder (M). Add 1–2 tablespoons of water (W), vinegar (Wd), ground paprika (F), and cream (E). Cook the sprouts for another 2 minutes until just – al dente.

Serves 2:
300 g (10 oz) Brussels sprouts
$1/4$ nutmeg
1 tbsp unsalted butter
pinch of curry powder
pinch of mustard powder
$1/2$ tbsp wine vinegar
pinch of ground paprika
2 tbsp cream

* Grating nutmeg made easy

Carefully halve the nutmeg then quarter it with a large knife. Place one quarter, cut side down, on a board. Using a small knife, shave it into very thin slices. This makes the flavour less pronounced.

power

YANG

PROMOTING

Apricots in

fruity, yang-promoting dessert

White Wine

Serves 2: • 8 ripe apricots • 250 ml (10 fl oz) white wine • sprig of marjoram • 1 vanilla pod • 2 tbsp dried

sugar cane juice (from a health-food store) • 1 chilli pod • sea salt • 1 unwaxed lemon

Wash the apricots. Place the wine (Wd), apricots (F), and marjoram (F) in a pan. Slit open the

vanilla pod and remove the pulp. Finely chop the pod. Add the vanilla (E), dried sugar cane juice

(E), chilli (M), and salt (W) to the pan. Wash and slice the lemon (Wd), add to the other

ingredients and simmer gently for 3 minutes (F). Remove the apricots and leave to cool. Reduce

the cooking liquid to a third.

YANG-PROMOTING

Lamb's Lettuce

strengthens the heart and lifts the mood

with Basil

Serves 2: • 200 g (7 oz) lamb's lettuce • 2 bunches of basil • 2 tbsp balsamic vinegar • 2 tbsp

olive oil • 1 tbsp cream • pepper • 1 tbsp water • sea salt

Thoroughly wash the lamb's lettuce, and drain. Wash and shake dry the basil, and

shred the leaves into large pieces. Place the vinegar (Wd), lamb's lettuce (F), basil (F),

oil (E), and cream (E) in a bowl. Combine with the pepper (M), water (W), and salt (W).

Arrange on plates.

YIN-PROMOTING

Buckwheat with Sage

plenty of strength for the heart

Dry roast the buckwheat (F) in a pan over a medium heat, stirring continuously, for about 10 minutes. Wash 12 sage leaves, pat dry, and chop.

Serves 2:
200 g (7 oz) buckwheat
24 sage leaves
1 onion
1 tbsp unsalted butter
pepper
200 ml (7 fl oz) vegetable stock
200 ml (7 fl oz) white wine
2 juniper berries
1 egg yolk
1 tbsp flour
2–3 tbsp oil for frying
1 tbsp olive oil

Peel and dice the onion. Combine the sage (F), butter (E), and diced onion (M) with the buckwheat. Season with pepper (M). Pour over the stock (W) and wine (Wd), and add the juniper berries (F). Simmer the buckwheat gently over a low heat for about 20 minutes.

For the batter, mix together the egg yolk (E) with the flour (E) until smooth. Heat the oil (E) in a frying pan. Coat the remaining sage leaves with the batter and fry over medium heat. Drain on paper towels. Arrange the buckwheat and sage leaves on plates, drizzle over the olive oil, and serve.

Sage

Due to its slightly bitter but pleasantly spicy flavour and relatively low moisture content, sage provides plenty of strength for the coronary heart circulation (heart and small intestine).

power

YANG
PROMOTING

Braised

strengthens your Earth element

Pumpkin

Remove the seeds and fibres from the pumpkin. Cut the flesh into chunks.

Wash and peel the potatoes, and cut into chunks. Peel and thinly slice the

onion.

Heat about 1 litre (2 pints) water (W) and the lemon

juice in a pot. Add the juniper berries (F), potatoes

(E), chopped pumpkin (E), sliced onion (M), salt (W),

lemon rind (Wd), ground paprika (F), and marjoram

(F). Cover with a lid and simmer gently over a low

heat for about 30 minutes.

Pour away any water left at the end of this time. Stir

in the butter (E) and cream (E). Season with pepper

(M), curry powder (M), and salt (W). Mash the

pumpkin coarsely with a potato masher.

Serves 2:
750 g (1 lb 10 oz) pumpkin
300 g (10 oz) floury potatoes
1 onion
1 tbsp lemon juice
4 juniper berries
pinch of sea salt
rind of 1 unwaxed lemon
pinch of ground paprika
1 sprig of marjoram
2 tbsp unsalted butter
4 tbsp cream
pepper
pinch of curry powder

Powerful pumpkin

Pumpkin flesh has a very high water content
and provides fibre, and thus helps digestion.
Pumpkin moistens and strengthens the Earth
element (stomach, spleen, and pancreas) in the best
possible way.

power

YIN

PROMOTING

Brown
refreshes and revitalizes when tired
Mushroom Salad

Wash and trim the mushrooms (E), and cut into wafer-thin slices. Fan the sliced mushrooms over two plates. Wash the carrot (E), peel, and cut lengthwise into thin slices. Cut the slices into very thin strips, then arrange over the mushrooms.

Sprinkle 1 tablespoon of olive oil (E) over each plate. Peel the shallot (M), finely chop, and sprinkle over the carrots. Season with pepper (M) and salt (W). Sprinkle ½ tablespoon of vinegar (Wd) over each. Finely chop a little lemon rind, and sprinkle over the salad with some paprika (F). Drizzle 1 tablespoon of pear juice (E) over each, garnish with the chopped chives (M), and serve.

Serves 2:
10 brown mushrooms
½ carrot
2 tbsp olive oil
1 shallot
pepper
sea salt
1 tbsp white wine vinegar
rind of 1 unwaxed lemon
pinch of ground paprika
2 tbsp pear juice
2 tbsp chopped chives

Ligurian olive oil

There are as many different flavours of olive oil as there are varieties. The range extends from gentle and mild through fruity to strong and dry. Anyone who does not normally like the flavour of olive oil will undoubtedly appreciate Ligurian olive oil, which is the mildest one of all.

power

YIN

PROMOTING

Lamb's Lettuce with
with mild olive oil from Liguria
Avocado and Mango

Wash the orange and dry well. Remove some of the rind with a zester. Peel the orange, removing the white pith as well. Remove the fruit segments from between the membranes. Wash the Little Gem lettuces and shred coarsely. Slit the tomatoes and dip in boiling water for a few seconds. Remove, then skin, halve, and remove the seeds and cores. Finely chop the tomatoes, reserving the juices. Wash and drain the lamb's lettuce. Wash and peel the carrot, and cut into fine strips. Peel the mango, remove the flesh from the stone, and cut into strips. Halve the avocado and remove the stone. Peel the avocado halves and slice. Peel and thinly slice the shallots. Trim and wash the spring onions, and slice diagonally. Combine the orange segments (Wd), Little Gems (Wd), tomatoes (Wd), lamb's lettuce (F), carrot strips (E), sliced mango (E), sliced avocado (E), olive oil (E), sliced shallots (M), and spring onions (M) in a bowl with salt (W), tomato juices (W), vinegar (Wd), crème fraîche (Wd), ground paprika (F), and cream (E).

Serves 2:

1 unwaxed orange
2 Little Gem lettuces
2 tomatoes
50 g (1 ³/₄ oz) lamb's lettuce
1 carrot
1 ripe mango
1 ripe avocado
2 shallots
3 tbsp Ligurian olive oil
bunch of spring onions
sea salt
2 tbsp balsamic vinegar
1 tbsp crème fraîche
pinch of ground paprika
2 tbsp cream

power

YIN-PROMOTING

Linguine with Vegetable Strips

also popular with children

Serves 2:

1 small courgette (zucchini)

1 carrot

1 parsnip

¹/₂ leek

sea salt

1 tbsp wine vinegar

250 g (9 oz) linguine

200 g (7 oz) Emmental cheese

3 tbsp cooked, sieved tomato
(or 'passata', ready-made)

pinch of ground paprika

1 tbsp unsalted butter

Wash and trim the courgette, and cut lengthwise into thin slices. Cut each slice into thin strips. Wash the carrot and parsnip, and peel. Cut lengthwise into thin slices, and cut the slices into strips. Halve the leek lengthwise and wash. Cut the halved leek lengthwise into thin strips.

Add the salt (W) and vinegar (Wd) to about 1 litre (2 pints) of water (W), and bring to a boil (F). Cook the linguine (E), courgette (E), carrot (E), parsnip (E), and leek (M) for 5–6 minutes. Meanwhile, grate the Emmental. Drain the vegetable pasta in a sieve, and season with salt (W). Combine the passata (Wd), ground paprika (F), and butter (E) with the vegetable pasta. Arrange on two plates, sprinkle over the cheese (E), and serve immediately.

power YIN-PROMOTING

Corn on the Cob

popular with all ages

with Parsnips

Serves 2:

4 parsnips

bunch of spring onions

4 corn on the cob

1 onion

10 peppercorns

1 tbsp wine vinegar

2 juniper berries

1 tbsp unsalted butter

pinch of curry powder

pepper

sea salt

4 cherry tomatoes

bunch of rocket

1 tbsp cream

Wash and peel the parsnips (E), and cut lengthwise into slices. Cut these slices into strips. Place the peel in a large saucepan. Wash and peel the spring onions, slice diagonally, then place to one side. Trim the corn on the cob (E) and add to the parsnip peel. Peel the onion (M) and add to the corn. Add the peppercorns (M), 1 litre (2 pints) of water (W), the vinegar (Wd), and the juniper berries (F), and cook gently for 20 minutes over a low heat. Leave the corn to cool, then scrape off the kernels.

Heat a pan and melt the butter (E). Fry the parsnips (E) for 4–5 minutes. Add the sweetcorn (E) and the spring onions (M). Season with the curry powder (M), pepper (M), and salt (W). Wash and quarter the tomatoes, and remove the core. Wash and chop the rocket. Add the tomatoes (Wd), rocket (F), and cream (E) to the pan, and simmer for about 1 minute. Arrange on plates and serve.

Parsnip

Parsnip is naturally sweet, and strengthens the stomach, spleen, and pancreas. You will avoid feeling ravenous if you satisfy your Earth element with enough natural sweetness, and so you should give priority to vegetables that are naturally sweet.

YANG

PROMOTING

power

Millet Salad with
restores the energy balance
Asparagus and Capers

Heat a saucepan over medium heat (F). Sprinkle in the millet (E) and dry roast for about 12 minutes, stirring continuously, until they are just steaming and starting to smell. Stir in the green pepper (M), vegetable stock (W), lemon rind (Wd), and the pesto (F). Turn off the heat, leaving the millet to absorb the cooking liquid for another 10 minutes.

Meanwhile, wash, trim, and carefully peel the asparagus (F), and cut each piece diagonally into three. Place the asparagus in a pan, add the butter (E), and fry over a medium heat for 3–4 minutes.

Place the millet and the asparagus in a bowl. Sprinkle over the olive oil (E), and season with the curry powder (M), pepper (M), and salt (W). Wash and quarter the tomatoes (Wd), remove the cores, and add to the bowl. Stir in the capers (F) and the cream (E). Arrange on plates and serve.

Serves 2:

300 g (10 oz) millet

2 tbsp green pepper

700 ml (1 ¼ pints) vegetable stock

rind of 1 unwaxed lemon

1 tbsp pesto (ready-made)

500 g (1 lb 2 oz) asparagus

1 tbsp unsalted butter

1 tbsp Ligurian olive oil

pinch of curry powder

pepper and sea salt

10 cherry tomatoes

1 tbsp capers (in oil)

1 tbsp cream

Millet

Millet is a typical food from the neutral-thermal range. It distributes energy on the Yin and Yang side, thereby balancing the energies. It stores energy when there is excess, and provides it when there is a shortfall.

YANG

PROMOTING

power

Fennel and
especially good for the spleen
Peppers

Wash and trim the fennel, then halve and cut into slices. Thinly peel the bell pepper, and halve. Remove the core, seeds, and membrane, and chop into small pieces. Wash and trim the carrot, then peel and dice it. Wash, peel, and dice the potato. Cut the leek into half lengthwise, wash, and cut into half rings. Peel and halve the shallot, and slice into half rings.

Heat a pan over a medium heat (F), and melt the butter (E). Braise the fennel (E), pepper (E), carrot (E), potato (E), leek (M), and shallot (M) for about 5 minutes. Pour over the stock (W), cover with a lid, and simmer for about 15 minutes. Stir in the lemon rind (Wd), crème fraîche (Wd), ground paprika (F), and cream (E). Season with pepper (M) and salt (W), and serve.

Serves 2:

1 large fennel bulb

1 red bell pepper (capsicum)

1 carrot

1 large potato

½ leek

1 shallot

1 tbsp unsalted butter

500 ml (20 fl oz) vegetable stock

rind of ½ unwaxed lemon

1 tbsp crème fraîche

pinch of ground paprika

1 tbsp cream

pepper

sea salt

power

Yang-promoting

Sweet-boiled
Water
the best elixir of life for the body

In a large pot, bring the water (W), the lemon rind (Wd), and the juniper berry (F) to a boil. Cover with a lid and boil over a medium heat for 15 minutes. Turn off the cooker, and leave the water for about 20 minutes until the minerals and salts have deposited on the bottom of the pot.

Keep the water hot in vacuum flasks, and drink throughout the day, either warm or at room temperature. It is the ideal way of providing fluid for the body, humidifying the lungs, and detoxifying the body by osmosis. If you would like to flavour the water, do so by adding fruit vinegar, soy sauce, sea vegetables, aniseed, or cardamom seeds.

Daily quantity for 2 people:
5 litres (10 pints) of water
rind of 1 unwaxed lemon
1 juniper berry

Miso soup for breakfast

Place 1–2 teaspoons miso paste (W) – obtainable from Asian supermarkets and health-food stores – in a cup. Add a few sea vegetables if you like, and stir with 2–3 tablespoons of sweet-boiled water until smooth. Top with hot sweet-boiled water, and sip. You can, if you like, flavour miso soup with horseradish, coriander leaves, or parsley.

power

YIN

PROMOTING

Saffron

ideal with vegetables

Rice

Serves 2: • 1 carrot • 1 parsnip • 1 shallot • 2 tbsp unsalted butter • 250 g (9 oz) Basmati rice • 1 star anise • 1 unwaxed lemon • saffron threads • pepper • sea salt

Wash, trim, and grate the carrot and parsnip. Peel and chop the shallot. Heat a pan (F), and melt 1 tablespoon of butter (E). Fry the parsnip (E), shallot (M), rice (M), and star anise (M) for 5 minutes. Pour over 1.5 litres (2 ½ pints) of water (W). Thinly peel the lemon, add the rind to the rice with the saffron (F), and cook for 10 minutes. Turn off the heat. Leave the rice to absorb the liquid for 6 minutes. Add the remaining butter, and season with pepper (M) and salt (W).

YIN-PROMOTING

Watercress

hearty and interesting

Salad

Serves 2: • 1 orange • ground paprika • cane sugar • 1 carrot • 2 bunches of watercress • bunch of spring onions • 1 tbsp wine vinegar • bunch of rocket • 1 tbsp unsalted butter • sea salt

Cut the rind from the orange, and cut the rind into strips. Squeeze the juice from the orange. Combine the paprika (F), sugar (E), and orange strips (E). Peel and grate the carrot. Wash and chop the watercress. Trim the spring onions and slice diagonally. Bring 100 ml (4 fl oz) water (W), vinegar (Wd), and orange juice (Wd) to a boil. Wash and chop the rocket (F). Add the butter (E), orange rind (E), carrots (E), watercress (M), and spring onions (M) to the liquid. Cook for 3 minutes, and season with salt.

YIN-PROMOTING

Stuffed
ideal moisture for the lungs
Spanish Onions

Preheat the oven to 150 °C (300 °F). Peel the onions, cut off the top to make a lid, and place the bases and lids in an ovenproof dish. Pour over 4 tablespoons of water (W) and add a little lemon rind (Wd). Place the onions in the bottom of the oven and bake for about 15 minutes (F). To make the filling, remove and finely chop the insides, and place in a bowl. Season with ground paprika (F). Finely chop the bread (E) and add to the chopped onion with the cream (E). Wash and shake dry the chives, then slice thinly and add to the onion. Season with pepper (M), coriander seeds (M), and salt (W). Wash and pick over the spinach (Wd), remove any coarse stalks, and chop the leaves. Finely chop the remaining lemon rind (Wd), and add the spinach and the lemon rind to the onion mixture. Spoon the filling into the onions, and place in the bottom of the oven (F) at about 120 °C/250 °F to cook for another 20 minutes.

Serves 2:

4 large Spanish onions
rind of ¹/₂ unwaxed lemon
pinch of ground paprika
slice of day-old bread
2 tbsp cream
bunch of chives
pepper
12 coriander seeds
sea salt
50 g (1 ³/₄ oz) fresh spinach

Spanish onions

From the thermal point of view, the Spanish onion is cold, and its juices moisturize the lung-large intestine circulation.

YIN

PROMOTING

power

Spicy

with peanut sauce – a popular Asian delicacy

Chicken Kebabs

Serves 2:

2 chicken breasts

4 garlic cloves

2 stalks of lemon grass

¹/₂ in (1 cm) piece of ginger

100 ml (4 fl oz) soy sauce

grated rind of 1 unwaxed lemon

2 tbsp pear juice

12 coriander seeds

1 star anise

4 wooden skewers

oil

1 tbsp unsalted butter

10 peppercorns

2 tbsp peanut butter

1 tbsp wine vinegar

pinch of ground paprika

2 tbsp cream

pepper

sea salt

Cut the chicken into bite-size pieces. Peel and finely chop the garlic (M), and place in a bowl with the chicken (M). Wash the lemon grass, and peel the ginger; cut both into slices. Combine the soy sauce (W), lemon rind (Wd), lemon grass (F), pear juice (E), coriander seeds (M), ginger (M), and star anise (M) with the chicken, and cover the bowl. Marinate the meat for at least 5 hours, stirring frequently.

Place the wooden skewers in the oil for a few minutes. Thread chicken, lemon grass, and ginger alternately on the skewers. Preheat the oven to 120 °C (250 °F).

Heat a pan over a low heat (F). Melt the butter (E), then add the peppercorns (M). Fry the chicken skewers for about 12 minutes, then remove and keep warm in the oven. Stir the peanut butter into the cooking juices, then add 200 ml (8 fl oz) water (W) and the marinade. Add the vinegar (Wd), ground paprika (F), and cream (E). Season the sauce with pepper (M) and salt (W), and serve with the skewers.

power

YANG-PROMOTING

Leeks
particularly good for the lungs and large intestine
with Potatoes

Wash, peel, and coarsely chop the potatoes and carrots. Trim the leek, cut in half lengthwise, then cut into half rings. Peel and coarsely chop the onion. Peel the garlic.

Serves 2:
4 large potatoes
2 carrots
2 leeks
1 onion
2 garlic cloves
4 pimento seeds
2 bay leaves
2 tbsp wine vinegar
sprig of tarragon
2 juniper berries
100 ml (4 fl oz) full cream milk
100 ml (4 fl oz) cream
¹/₂ tbsp unsalted butter
pepper and sea salt

Place the potatoes (E), carrots (E), leek (M), and onions (M) in a pot. Add the pimento seeds (M), garlic (M), bay leaves (M), 1 litre (2 pints) of water (W), vinegar (Wd), tarragon (Wd), and juniper berries (F) to the vegetables in the pot, and bring to a boil. Cook over a low heat for 20 minutes.

Pour off the water. Add the milk (E), cream (E), and butter (E) to the cooked vegetables. Roughly mash with a potato masher. Season with pepper (M) and salt (W). Arrange the vegetables on plates, and serve.

power

Leek

This member of the allium family provides strength for the lungs and large intestine. Finely mashed with a little added liquid, it also provides moisture for the body.

YANG

PROMOTING

Celeriac Strips
a culinary delight
on Turnips

Preheat the oven to 120 °C (280 °F). Wash and peel the celeriac, cut into chunks, and then slice into julienne strips, either by hand or using an electric slicer. Squeeze the lemon. Season (W) the celeriac strips (M) with salt (W), and sprinkle with all but 1 tablespoon of the lemon juice (Wd). Season with ground paprika (F). Place the celeriac strips in the bottom of the oven (100 °C/210 °F) for about 1 ¼ hours to dry. Wash, peel, and halve or quarter the turnips. Peel the garlic, and peel and quarter the shallot.

Heat a pan over medium heat (F), and melt the butter (E). Braise the turnips (M) with the garlic (M) and quartered shallot (M) for 5 minutes. Season with pepper (M). Pour over the vegetable stock (W) and the remaining lemon juice (Wd). Stir in the crème fraîche (Wd), season with ground paprika (F), and cook. Arrange the celeriac strips and the turnips on plates, and serve.

Serves 2:
1 celeriac
1 lemon
sea salt
pinch of ground paprika
8 turnips
1 garlic clove
1 shallot
1 tbsp unsalted butter
white pepper
100 ml (4 fl oz) vegetable stock
1 tbsp crème fraîche

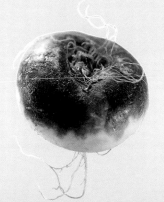

Turnips

Turnips and celeriac are an unbeatable combination. From the thermal aspect, turnips, or the French version *navettes*, are cold and provide moisture, while the dried celeriac provides strength for the lungs and intestine, and new energy.

YANG

PROMOTING

power

Catfish in Root

strengthens the kidneys

Vegetable Stock

Wash and peel the carrots (E) and the parsnips (E), cut into slices, and cut the slices into strips. Trim the leek (M), halve lengthwise, then wash and cut into strips. Peel the celeriac (M) and cut into strips. Peel the shallots and garlic. Thinly slice the shallots. Place the vegetable strips (E/M) and shallot slices (M) in a saucepan with 10 coriander seeds (M) and the garlic (M). Just cover the vegetables with water (W). Place the catfish on top, and salt (W). Add the vinegar (Wd) and the juniper berries (F). Preheat the oven to 70 °C (160 °F). Cook the vegetables and the fish in the oven for 8–9 minutes.

Keep the fish warm. Boil the vegetable liquid for 30 minutes. Stir in the butter (E), cream (E), the remaining coriander seeds (M), and the mustard (M). Season with pepper (M) and salt (W).

Serves 2:
4 carrots
2 parsnips
1 leek
piece of celeriac
2 shallots
2 garlic cloves
1 tsp coriander seeds
300 g (10 oz) catfish
sea salt
1 tbsp white wine vinegar
4 juniper berries
1 tbsp unsalted butter
2 tbsp cream
1 tbsp Dijon mustard
pepper

✳ Catfish

This freshwater fish is widely farmed, and invariably of good quality. Find out whether there is a farm in your area. If not, and you buy it from a fishmonger, make sure that the fish really is fresh. Catfish strengthens the kidneys and the bladder.

YIN

PROMOTING

power

Lentil Soup

even better with browned butter

with Rosemary

Serves 2:
200 g (7 oz) brown lentils
1 tbsp wine vinegar
4 juniper berries
sprig of rosemary
2 potatoes
2 carrots
1 large onion
¹/₂ leek
pepper and sea salt
1 tbsp crème fraîche
pinch of ground paprika
2 tbsp cream

Place the lentils (W) in a dish, cover with plenty of water (W), and leave overnight. Places the lentils and the water in a pan, and pour over 1 litre (2 pints) of water. Add the vinegar (Wd), juniper berries (F), and rosemary (F), and simmer gently over a low heat for about 1 hour.

Meanwhile, wash, peel, and dice the potatoes and carrots. Trim and wash the leek, and cut into rings. Add the potatoes (E), carrots (E), onion (M) and leek (M) to the soup. Season with pepper (M), and simmer for another 20 minutes.

Stir in the salt (W), crème fraîche (Wd), ground paprika (F) and cream (E). Ladle into deep bowls, and serve with browned butter if desired.

power

Yin-promoting

Braised

sage adds a special touch

Red Cabbage

Remove the outer leaves and the core from the red cabbage (W). Cut the cabbage into quarters, slice the quarters, and place in a pot. Shave the nutmeg with the blade of a knife. Peel and quarter the shallots. Add 2 tablespoons of vinegar (Wd), the white wine (Wd), ground paprika (F), nutmeg (F), and sage leaves to the cabbage.

Heat over a low heat. Then add the butter (E), cream (E), pimento (M) and coriander seeds (M), bay leaves (M), shallot quarters (M), clove (M), and cinnamon (M). Cover with a lid, and simmer gently for 20 minutes, stirring occasionally.

Meanwhile, wash and shake dry the parsley, and chop. Finally, season the red cabbage with salt (W), crème fraîche (Wd) and 1 tbsp vinegar (Wd). Sprinkle with the parsley (Wd), and serve.

Serves 2:
- 1/2 red cabbage
- 1/2 nutmeg
- 4 shallots
- 3 tbsp balsamic vinegar
- glass of white wine
- 1 tsp ground paprika
- 8 sage leaves
- 2 tbsp unsalted butter
- 2 tbsp cream
- 6 pimento seeds
- 12 coriander seeds
- 3 bay leaves
- 1 clove
- pinch of ground cinnamon
- sea salt
- 1 tbsp crème fraîche
- 1/2 bunch flat-leafed parsley

power

YIN-PROMOTING

Chickpea Purée
ideal on bread
with Sesame

Soak the chickpeas (W) overnight in plenty of water. Next day, simmer the chickpeas and soaking water, lemon juice (Wd), and ground paprika (F)

Serves 2:
200 g (7 oz) chickpeas
1 tbsp lemon juice
pinch of ground paprika
2 garlic cloves
bunch of flat-leafed parsley
olive oil
pepper
100 g (3 ¹/₂ oz) sesame seeds
sea salt
4–6 slices cucumber
2 tbsp black olives

over a low heat for 1 hour, then leave to cool. Meanwhile, peel the garlic. Wash and shake dry the parsley, and remove the florets from the stalks.

Purée 4 tablespoons of olive oil (E), the garlic (M), pepper (M), sesame seeds (W), chickpeas (W), salt (W), and parsley (Wd) in the blender until smooth. Arrange the purée on plates, making a well in the middle. Garnish with the cucumber slices (Wd) and olives (F), and sprinkle over the ground paprika (F). Pour olive oil into the well if liked. Goes well with toasted flat bread.

Skin chickpeas – it's worth it

The chickpea purée is more delicate if the skins are removed from the chickpeas before they are puréed. Although this is tedious, it is well worth the effort.

power

YIN

PROMOTING

Fennel Purée with
crispy, yet as smooth as butter
Eggplant Chips

Wash, peel, and dice the potatoes. Wash and trim the fennel, then halve and cut into strips. Wash, peel, and slice the carrots. Peel the onion and the garlic. Dice the onion. Melt 1 tablespoon of butter in a pot. Place the potatoes (E), fennel (E), carrots (E), onions (M), peppercorns (M), 1 garlic clove (M), curry powder (M), 300 ml (12 fl oz) water (W), vinegar (Wd), and ground paprika (F) in a pot, and cook over a low heat for 25 minutes.

Meanwhile, wash and trim the eggplant, and cut into thin slices. Add the remaining butter (E) to the vegetables, and mash them. Season with pepper (M) and salt (W).

Heat a pan (F), and pour in the oil (E). Add the remaining garlic clove (M). Fry the eggplant slices until crispy, then season with salt (W). Arrange the purée on plates, dip the eggplant chips in the purée, and serve.

Serves 2:
2 potatoes
2 fennel bulbs
4 carrots
1 onion
3 garlic cloves
2 tbsp unsalted butter
6 peppercorns
pinch of curry powder
1 tbsp wine vinegar
pinch of ground paprika
1 medium eggplant (aubergine)
pepper
sea salt
2 tbsp oil for frying

power
YANG-PROMOTING

Skin-fried

delicious with fresh or salt-water perch

Perch

Wash the fish, pat dry with paper towels, and score the skin. Divide the fillets. Preheat the oven to 70 °C (160 °F). Heat a cast-iron pan over a low heat (F), and melt the butter (E). Grate the pepper (M) over the butter, and tilt the pan from side to side. Place the fish fillets (W), skin side down, in the pan, and fry this side only for 8 minutes. Season the skin side with salt (W), and keep warm, skin side up.

Meanwhile, wash and trim the fennel, and cut into strips. Wash and shake dry the rocket, and tear into pieces. Pour the fish stock (W) into the pan, and stir in the crème fraîche (Wd). Braise the rocket (F) and the fennel (E) in the sauce. Season with curry powder (M), pepper (M), and salt (W). Pour the sauce onto two plates. Place the fish, skin side up, on the sauce, and serve.

Serves 2:

300 g (10 oz) perch fillets, with skin
1 tbsp unsalted butter
pepper and sea salt
2 fennel bulbs
bunch of rocket
100 ml (4 fl oz) fish stock (ready-made)
2 tbsp crème fraîche
pinch of curry powder

Perfect results

In this method, the fish is cooked on one side only. It is ready when a glassy line can just be seen at the highest (i.e. fleshiest) point. As it cooks, you can watch how the fish cooks from the bottom up.

YANG

PROMOTING

power

Terrine of

delicious as a starter

Smoked Trout

Remove the skin from the smoked fish (W), then pick out the bones and place in a bowl. Mash lightly with a fork. Wash and shake dry the parsley, then remove the florets from the stalks and chop very finely. Peel and finely chop the shallot. Soft-boil the eggs for 4 minutes, hold under cold water, and peel.

Then add the lemon juice (Wd), crème fraîche (Wd), parsley (Wd), ground paprika (F), and butter (E) to the fish. Halve the eggs and add the soft yolks to the fish. Season well with pepper (M), curry powder (M), the chopped shallot (M), and salt (W).

Mash again with a fork, and combine well. Place the fish mixture in a loaf pan or ramekins, and place in the refrigerator for 2 hours.

Serves 2:

2 freshly smoked river char or trout
bunch of flat-leafed parsley
1 shallot
4 eggs
1 tbsp lemon juice
2 tbsp crème fraîche
ground paprika
1 tbsp unsalted butter
pepper
curry powder
sea salt

The fresher the fish ...

The terrine is even more delicious if the fish is absolutely fresh, and still warm from being smoked. If you like, you can warm the fish in the oven for a few moments before you make the terrine.

YANG

PROMOTING

Index

Feng Shui Cooking

Abbreviations:

tsp = teaspoon
tbsp = tablespoon

Most of the ingredients required for the recipes in this book are available from supermarkets, delicatessens and health food stores. For more information, contact the following importers of organic produce:-
The Organic Food Company, Unit 2, Blacknest Industrial Estate, Blacknest Road, Alton GU34 4PX; (T) 01420 520530 (F) 01420 23985
Windmill Organics, 66 Meadow Close, London SW20 9JD
(T) 0208 395 9749 (F) 0208 286 4732

Fermented wheat juice is produced in Germany by Kanne Brottrunk GMBH
(T) 00 49 2592 97400 (F) 00 49 2592 61370

Further information on German food importers is available from The Central Marketing Organisation (T) 0208 944 0484
(F) 0208 944 0441

First published in the UK by
Gaia Books Ltd, 20 High Street,
Stroud, GL5 1AZ

Registered at 66 Charlotte St,
London W1P 1LR
Originally published under the title
Feng Shui in der Küche

© Gräfe und Unzer Verlag GmbH
Munich. English translation copyright
© 2000 Gaia Books Ltd
Translated by Mo Croasdale in association
with First Edition Translations Ltd,
Cambridge, UK.

Reproduction: MRM Graphics Ltd,
Winslow, UK.
Printed in Singapore by Imago

ISBN 1 85675 146 5

A catalogue record for this book is available in
the British Library

10 9 8 7 6 5 4 3 2 1

Caution
The techniques and recipes in this book
are to be used at the reader's sole
discretion and risk.
Always consult a doctor if you are in doubt
about a medical condition.

Günther Sator
Günther Sator is one of the first European
experts to specialise in adapting Feng Shui
to our Western culture. He is now one of the
leading consultants to the banking industry,
and corporate and private clients. He is
author of several best-selling books on the
subject of Feng Shui.

Ilse-Maria Fahrnow is a doctor of and lecturer
in TCM, homeopathy, and naturopathy.

Jürgen Fahrnow is a TCM dietetics advisor,
cook, restaurant manager, and sommelier.

Photographs: FoodPhotography Eising, Munich

Susie M. and **Pete Eising** have studios in
Munich and Kennebunkport, Maine/USA.
They studied at the Munich Academy of
Photography, where they established their
own studio for food photography in 1991.

Feng Shui Cooking
Recipes for harmony and
health
Fahrnow, Fahrnow and Sator
£4.99
ISBN 1 85675 146 5
More energy and wellbeing
from recipes that balance
your food.

Beauty Food
The natural way to looking
good
Dagmar von Cramm
£4.99
ISBN 1 85675 141 4
Natural beauty for skin and
hair - eating routines for a
fabulous complexion.

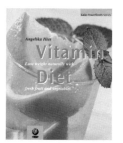

Vitamin Diet
Lose weight naturally with
fresh fruit and vegetables
Angelika Ilies
£4.99
ISBN 1 85675 145 7
All the benefits of eating fresh
fruit and vegetables plus a
natural way to weight loss.

Low Cholesterol - Low Fat
The easy way to reduce
cholesterol, stay slim and
enjoy your food
Döpp, Willrich and Rebbe
£4.99
ISBN 1 85675 166 X
Stay fit, slim and healthy
with easy-to-prepare
gourmet feasts.

Energy Drinks
Power-packed juices, mixed,
shaken or stirred
Friedrich Bohlmann
£4.99
ISBN 1 85675 140 6
Fresh juices packed full of
goodness for vitality and
health.

Anti Stress
Recipes for acid-alkaline
balance
Dagmar von Cramm
£4.99
ISBN 1 85675 155 4
A balanced diet to reduce
stress levels, maximise
immunity and help you
keep fit.

Detox
Foods to cleanse and purify
from within
Angelika Ilies
£4.99
ISBN 1 85675 150 3
Detoxify your body as part of
your daily routine by eating
nutritional foods that have
cleansing properties.

Mood Food
Recipes to cheer you up,
revitalize and comfort you
Marlisa Szwillus
£4.99
ISBN 1 85675 161 9
The best soul comforters,
the quickest revitalizers
and the most satisfying
stress busters.

To order the books featured on this page call 01453 752985, fax 01453 752987 with your credit/debit card details, or
send a cheque made payable to Gaia Books to Gaia Books Ltd., 20 High Street, Stroud, Glos., GL5 1AZ.
e-mail: gaiapub@dircon.co.uk or visit our website www.gaiabooks.co.uk

Suitable foods for a five-element diet

Element	Hot	Warm
Wood	Vinegar essence, shellfish and crustaceans	Vinegar, leeks, hazelnuts, raspberry, cherries, pork and lamb liver
Fire	Nutmeg, saffron, juniper berries, grilled meat	Basil, marjoram, cocoa, ... buckwheat, amaranth, almonds, apricots, lamb a... goat meat, tea, coffee, Brussels sprouts
Earth	Aniseed, fennel, honey, liquorice, dried sugar cane juice, liquors	Malt, vanilla, spelt, gluten... rice, fennel, bell peppers (capsicum), beef
Metal	Chilli, curry, white pepper, cinnamon, garlic, star anise, pimento, venison	Ginger, coriander, bay leaf, clove, leeks, black pepper, mustard, thyme, chives, chicken, venison
Water	Ham and salami, trout, char, salmon, whitefish, shellfish and crustaceans, salt	Cumin, pumpkin seeds, sesame, eggplant (aubergine), pork, pigeon, eel, mackerel, sturgeon, tuna